BRILLIANT WOMEN

INCREDIBLE SPORTING CHAMPIONS

Written by Georgia Amson-Bradshaw
Illustrated by Rita Petruccioli

BARRON'S

CONTENTS

Incredible Sporting Champions	3
Marie Marvingt	5
Babe Didrikson Zaharias	9
Cathy Freeman	13
Sarah Storey	17
Serena Williams	21
Marta	25
Tatyana McFadden	29
Katie Ledecky	33
More Sporting Heroines	37
Get Involved in Sports!	44
Glossary	46
Further Information	47
Index	48

INCREDIBLE SPORTING CHAMPIONS

Imagine a soccer player running as fast as possible down the field—sweating, muddy, muscles working at full strength, skillfully maneuvering the ball. Eyes fixed on the goal, grimacing with effort, focused on taking down the opponent and winning—nothing else. At the last moment, she pivots, shoots—and scores!

Did that last sentence change the picture you had built up in your mind?

For many people the word "she" feels unexpected. Even today, the idea of a tough, competitive sporting champion is still largely presented to us as a man rather than a woman and that can stick unhelpfully in our minds.

Women's sports are more popular today than they have ever been, in terms of taking part and watching others play. They are finally starting to get at least some of the respect and the funding that they deserve, but it's a slow process. Female athletes still make far less money than male athletes and get fewer opportunities to reach their full potential with top-class professional training, resources, and big competitions that get lots of media coverage.

She can't play in a dress!

Throughout history, women and girls have been given all sorts of ridiculous reasons why they shouldn't enjoy sports just like men do. They're too fragile, it's bad for their health, they're not good enough to bother trying, they're not strong enough, it's just not "ladylike" (whatever that is supposed to mean these days) . . .

In this book you will meet just a few of the incredibly talented, dedicated, and brave women who have refused to let people decide for them what they are capable of achieving. They have often not received the respect and the fame they deserve—in many cases, they've been laughed at, called names, and struggled to even be allowed to take part in the sports to which they've dedicated their lives.

Read about athletes from many different sports, including tennis, running, swimming, boxing, cycling, gymnastics— even sword fighting and skateboarding! The sporting champions and pioneers in this book show that women can excel at any kind of sport, so let their stories inspire you.

Whether you already live for sports or are just starting to catch the bug, this book is full of ideas and tips to help you think and play like a pro. You might just be the next sporting champion. Read on to be inspired by these brilliant women in sports!

MARIE MARVINGT

Marie Marvingt never accepted any limits put on her as a woman, from disguising herself as a man to serve in the army to cycling the Tour de France route despite being excluded from the men-only race.

ALL-AROUNDER

Marie Marvingt swam, canoed, cycled, climbed, skied, skated, and flew her way into history with a huge range of impressive sporting "firsts" for women.

LIVED:	February 20, 1875–December 14, 1963
BORN IN:	Aurillac (France)
COMPETED FOR:	France and herself

Marie was required to take care of the house for her father and brother, after her mother died when she was just 14 years old. But her head was always full of dreams of adventure, and she read lots of books about explorers. Ignoring her dull, household duties, at the age of 15 she canoed over 248 mi (400 km) from Nancy, France to Koblenz, Germany.

She loved the challenge of long-distance events, and in 1905 she became the first woman to swim the length of the River Seine in Paris. The press called her "the red amphibian" because of her red bathing suit and impressive ability in the water.

Marie dominated the French winter sports seasons (which include events such as skiing, ice skating, and bobsledding) from 1908 to 1910, winning first place on 20 occasions. She was an avid cyclist, but was refused entry to the 1908 Tour de France because she was a woman. Not put off that easily, she cycled the course after the race had finished. In doing so, she completed a ride that only 36 out of the 114 men in the race had managed to finish that year—and her time would have beaten some of the men's times in the official race. Even today, the Tour de France is a men-only event.

During World War I (1914–1918), Marie disguised herself as a man and attempted to fight on the frontline. She was discovered and ended up serving as a nurse and pilot, becoming the first woman to fly combat missions. After the war she was awarded the Croix de Guerre (War Cross) for her achievements, and she campaigned for the introduction of air ambulances.

She was the first woman to climb many of the mountains in the French Alps, and the first woman to cross the English Channel in a hot-air balloon. Due to her risk-taking exploits, Marie was given the nickname "The Fiancée of Danger," which she loved and used for the title of her autobiography. In addition to the sports she won medals for, she had a wide range of sporting hobbies, such as martial arts, boxing, and even trapeze!

The French Academy of Sport awarded Marie a Medaille d'Or (gold medal) for her accomplishments in all sports. It is the only multi-sport medal that the Academy has ever awarded. Finally, at the age of 86, two years before her death, Marie cycled between Nancy and Paris—a distance of over 198 mi (320 km).

EMBRACE ADVENTURE LIKE MARIE

Marie Marvingt had an exciting life full of challenges and adventures, from her teenage years right up until the end of her life. Imagine that someone is writing a newspaper article about you, 20 years from now. What amazing adventures have you already had? Where have you been? What have you done? And what are you planning to do next? It's your life, so think big!

BABE DIDRIKSON ZAHARIAS

Babe Didrikson Zaharias took on any new challenge with confidence and flair. When she was once asked if there was anything she did not play, she shot back: "Yeah, dolls."

ALL-AROUNDER

With her almost unbelievable range of achievements in golf, basketball, baseball, and athletics, Babe has been described as the most talented athlete, male or female, ever seen in the USA.

LIVED:	June 26, 1911–September 27, 1956
BORN IN:	Port Arthur, Texas (USA)
COMPETED FOR:	Her employer, the USA, and herself

Babe's real name was Mildred Didrikson, but she got her nickname in a childhood baseball game where she was so impressive that people started calling her "Babe Ruth" after the male baseball legend. In high school she was the star of the basketball, tennis, golf, baseball, swimming, and volleyball teams.

Babe's first job after she left school was as a secretary, but she was only really employed so that she could play for the company's basketball team, the Golden Cyclones. She once represented the company in a women's team athletics championship as a team of one. She sprinted between the different events, and won the competition with more points than the total scored by the team of 22 women that came in second place!

Babe competed at the 1932 Olympic Games in the only three events that women were allowed to enter at the time. She won gold for the 80-m hurdles and for javelin, breaking two world records in the process. She won silver for high jump, missing out on a clean sweep of gold medals, after one of her jumps was ruled illegal because her head had cleared the bar before her body—this rule no longer exists.

After the Olympics, Babe was a celebrity, but there were no real opportunities for professional female athletes. So she toured the USA performing a variety show as "The World's Greatest Woman Athlete." This earned her a lot of money—around $1,200 a week in a time when the average woman earned a few cents an hour. Although she was paid well, she was often mocked and criticized in newspapers, with some writers saying that it wasn't "nice" for a woman to play sports, that she only did it because she was too ugly to find a husband, and that she must be a man in disguise.

In 1935, Babe decided to focus on golf, and it was in this sport that she most excelled. She practiced by hitting as many as 1,000 golf balls a day, and kept going until her hands were so raw with blisters that she had to bandage them! Babe dominated women's golf through the 1930s and 1940s, with a total of 82 tournament wins. By 1950 she had won every possible women's golf championship in the USA. She made history by qualifying and doing extremely well in a number of men's golf competitions, too. Babe was diagnosed with cancer in 1953. She won five more golf tournaments before her death at the age of just 45.

COMPETE LIKE BABE

Babe Didrikson Zaharias had a huge amount of confidence in herself and her athletic abilities, and she tried to enter every competition she could—even when, as a woman, she wasn't welcomed! Entering sports competitions is good practice and can be really fun. Find out what competitions you can enter at school, or through sports clubs in your local area.

CATHY FREEMAN

Cathy made history when she became the first Australian indigenous woman to win an international medal in any sport.

RUNNER

Cathy's talent is sprinting. She competed in several sprint events, including the 100 m, 200 m, 100-m relay, and her best event, the 400 m.

BORN: February 16, 1973

BORN IN: Mackay, Queensland (Australia)

COMPETED FOR: Australia

Cathy was born to Norman and Cecelia Freeman in 1973. Her dad and her grandfather had both been gifted sportsmen, but due to the laws governing what indigenous Australian people were and were not allowed to do, her grandfather had been prevented from developing his rugby league career abroad.

During much of the 20th century, indigenous Australians did not have the same rights as nonindigenous people. They were forced to live in certain places, and families were often forcibly split up, with children taken away from their parents.

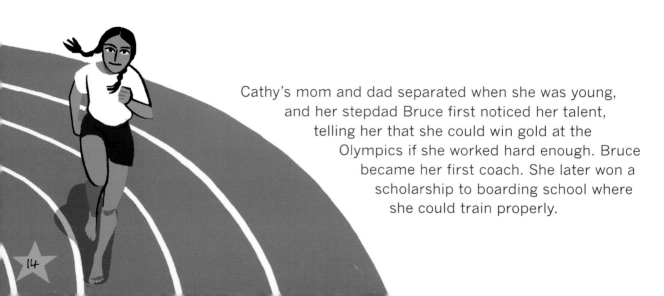

Cathy's mom and dad separated when she was young, and her stepdad Bruce first noticed her talent, telling her that she could win gold at the Olympics if she worked hard enough. Bruce became her first coach. She later won a scholarship to boarding school where she could train properly.

In 1990, Cathy was picked to join Australia's 4 × 100-m relay team for the 1990 Commonwealth Games. Her team won the gold medal, making Cathy the first-ever Aboriginal Commonwealth Games gold medalist at just 16 years old.

In 1996, Cathy competed in the 400 m at the Olympic Games in Atlanta, USA, winning silver. In 1997, she injured her foot, and had to take a year off to recover, but by 2000 she was back to full fitness. This was just in time for the Olympic Games that were held on her home turf, in Sydney, Australia. Cathy was chosen to light the Olympic cauldron at the opening ceremony.

She was determined to win gold this time, on behalf of her fellow Australians, and in particular, the Aboriginal people. When she won the 400-m race with a time of 49.11 seconds, she fell to her knees with relief, before doing a victory lap with both the Australian and Aboriginal flags.

Since retiring from competitive sports in 2003, Cathy has set up an organization that works to improve education for children in several remote Australian indigenous communities. Although Australian indigenous people now have the same rights according to the law as nonindigenous people, there is still inequality in educational achievement, which the Cathy Freeman Foundation aims to help address.

RUN LIKE CATHY

Cathy ran barefoot for much of her childhood. Barefoot running requires a slightly different running style. In barefoot running, when your foot hits the ground, it's important to land on the ball of your foot rather than your heel to protect your joints. Try running slowly and paying attention to what part of your foot hits the ground first. Is it your heel or another part of your foot? Do you land on the outside or the inside of your foot? Try simple exercises like jumping up and down in place, and balancing on each leg in turn, to increase the level of control you have over the muscles in your feet and legs.

SARAH STOREY

Sarah is the most successful British Paralympian of all time, with a total of 14 gold medals. She also holds an amazing 72 world records.

SWIMMER AND CYCLIST

An outstanding athlete, Sarah began in the pool, collecting many medals and records in swimming before switching to cycling to continue her winning streak.

BORN: October 26, 1977

BORN IN: Manchester (UK)

COMPETES FOR: England and Great Britain

Despite being born without a working left hand, Sarah was a very active child who loved all sports. Watching the Olympics at age seven, she knew she wanted to be an athlete, and by the time she was 10 she'd chosen swimming as her main sport. Her parents were supportive and she began to train seriously. At just 14 years old she competed for Great Britain in the Paralympic Games in Barcelona. She won an amazing two gold, three silver, and one bronze medals in the pool.

Ha! Your hair is wet!

Sarah may have been an internationally successful athlete, but school was a different matter. She was bullied by other girls, who would tease her for showing up with wet hair after training, and would move the chairs and tables at lunchtime so Sarah had nowhere to sit. Sarah stopped eating lunch to avoid the bullies, which made her lose a lot of weight. Eventually her mother intervened, and Sarah began to regain her weight and her confidence.

Brilliant observation, genius.

She represented Great Britain as a swimmer at three more Paralympic Games, winning a further three gold, five silver, and two bronze medals, until persistent ear infections forced her to switch sports. In 2005, Sarah became a cyclist instead. At her first international cycling event, the Para-cycling European Championships, she won triple gold. Then, in the Beijing Paralympics in 2008, she won gold in the individual pursuit with a time that also put her in the top eight of the Olympic finals, as well as winning the road time trial.

Just eight days after winning Paralympic gold, Sarah competed in the British Cycling National Track Championships against able-bodied cyclists, where she won the individual pursuit. She went on to become the first para-cyclist to compete for England at the Commonwealth Games against able-bodied cyclists.

At the London 2012 Paralympics, Sarah won gold in all four of her events, and also set a world record in the pursuit. She continued her winning streak at the Rio Paralympic Games in 2016, winning three gold medals. This secured her position as Great Britain's most decorated female Paralympian of all time.

LEARN SPORTS LIKE SARAH

When Sarah was forced to switch to cycling from swimming, she started off by watching professional cyclists on TV and in live races to observe their techniques. Try doing the same with your favorite sport. For example, if you like cycling, look at the riding position of professional cyclists during races. How do they have their bikes set up? If you like running, watch whether the athletes are taking long or short strides, and what they do with their arms.

SERENA WILLIAMS

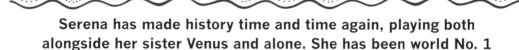

Serena has made history time and time again, playing both alongside her sister Venus and alone. She has been world No. 1 for 318 weeks in her career—more than six years.

TENNIS WORLD-CHAMPION

Serena Williams has the third fastest serve ever recorded in women's tennis, but her consistent strength, speed, and accuracy make her the most successful player of her time.

BORN:	September 26, 1981
BORN IN:	Saginaw, Michigan (USA)
COMPETES FOR:	USA

Serena and her sister Venus grew up in a family of five girls in southern Los Angeles, California. Their father, Richard, decided that women's tennis was a way for his five daughters to earn money and escape the poverty of their neighborhood in Compton (in Los Angeles). He bought instructional tennis books and videos, and drew up a plan to turn his daughters into professional tennis players.

Serena began playing tennis at just four years of age, and was coached intensively by her father on the poor-quality public courts in their local area. The courts were uneven and full of potholes, and there were threats of violence from gang members who hung around by the courts.

OK, Serena, try that again with more backspin.

When Serena was nine, the family moved to Florida so she and Venus could attend a prestigious tennis academy. Her father stopped the girls from entering junior tournaments for several years so they could focus on school and be protected from the intense competition and racism that he saw at these matches.

Serena began winning major championships in 1999, when she was still a teenager, and by the end of the year she was ranked the 4th best women's tennis player in the world. She moved up the ranks and became World Number One in women's tennis in 2002. She once held this position for 186 consecutive weeks—that's over three-and-a-half years!

Serena has won all of the most important world tennis competitions, known as the four "Grand Slams." In 2002–2003 and 2014–2015 she won all four of the Grand Slams in the same year.

As well as competing individually, Serena and Venus often play together in tennis doubles, and have never been beaten when playing together in a Grand Slam doubles final. They also share an Olympic record of each having won four Olympic gold medals, one in women's singles and three in women's doubles.

In 2017, Serena beat Venus in the Australian Open Final, winning her 23rd Grand Slam title. She later revealed that she had been around eight weeks pregnant at the time of her victory.

PRACTICE LIKE SERENA

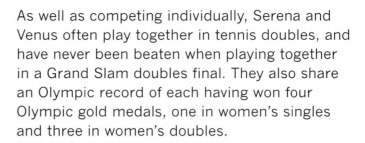

Serena Williams is an incredibly talented player, but that means nothing without lots and lots of hard work. Ever since she was a young girl, Serena has practiced the same movements over and over again, getting better and better each time. Whatever sport you like to do, think about the main movements you make and act them out in slow motion. Concentrate on what your body is doing at each stage of the movement. If you are serving a tennis ball, think about how you are throwing the ball up in the air to hit it—how fast, how high, how far from your body. Find the version of the movement that works best for you, and do it again and again.

MARTA

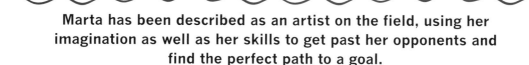

Marta has been described as an artist on the field, using her imagination as well as her skills to get past her opponents and find the perfect path to a goal.

SOCCER SUPERSTAR

Considered the most skillful women's soccer player in the world, Marta Vieira da Silva has reached the superstar heights of being known by her first name alone.

BORN: February 19, 1986

BORN IN: Dois Riachos, Alagoas (Brazil)

COMPETES FOR: Various clubs including Vasco de Gama, Umeå IK, and Brazil national team

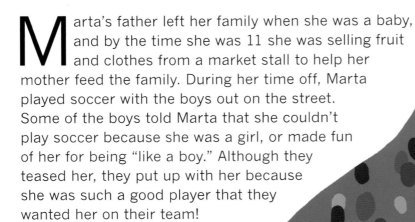

Marta's father left her family when she was a baby, and by the time she was 11 she was selling fruit and clothes from a market stall to help her mother feed the family. During her time off, Marta played soccer with the boys out on the street. Some of the boys told Marta that she couldn't play soccer because she was a girl, or made fun of her for being "like a boy." Although they teased her, they put up with her because she was such a good player that they wanted her on their team!

At 14, Marta was discovered by a well-known female soccer coach and left home to play for Vasco de Gama football club in Rio de Janeiro. She traveled for three days by bus to reach the city from her family home in the northeast. With professional coaching, she excelled and became part of the Brazilian teams that competed at the 2002 Under-19 World Championship and 2003 FIFA Women's Cup.

When she was 18, Marta joined Umeå IK soccer club in Sweden and the team went on to win the UEFA Europa League that year. She became the youngest woman to ever win the FIFA World Player of the Year Award when she was 20, and has since won this award four more times, as well as a huge range of other awards and honors.

Marta is considered part of the Brazilian tradition of skillful players such as Pelé, Ronaldinho, and Rivaldo. She has been the star of the Brazil national team, making 101 appearances for them and scoring a total of 105 goals. Only one soccer player in the world, Germany's Miroslav Klose, has scored more goals than her in World Cup matches—16 to her 15. Pelé scored 12 World Cup goals over his career.

Even for one of the best players in the world, it can be difficult to make a steady living in women's soccer. Many of the teams that Marta has joined have had money problems and have gone bankrupt. Although she is the highest-paid female soccer player in the world, she still makes a fraction of what the highest-paid male soccer players make.

PLAY LIKE MARTA

Marta likes to trick her opponents into thinking she is going to run one way with the ball, and then she speeds off past them in the opposite direction. Try it for yourself by turning your body in one direction as you approach your opponent, faking like you're about to kick the ball past them. Then suddenly lift your leg over the ball and turn the other way—using your other foot to kick the ball away ahead of you. Check out UEFA's Star Skills videos at *uefa.com/women/video* and learn tips, tricks, and techniques from Marta and other world-class players.

TATYANA McFADDEN

Tatyana McFadden has incredible upper-body strength, using her powerful arms to propel herself forward in her wheelchair to reach great speed in races.

WHEELCHAIR RACER

Tatyana has become a champion racer over long and short distances, not believing in putting limits on what she can achieve.

BORN: April 21, 1989

BORN IN: Russia, moved to USA at age 6, now an American citizen

COMPETES FOR: USA

Tatyana was born paralyzed from the waist down. Her birth mother couldn't look after her, so Tatyana went to live in an orphanage. The orphanage couldn't afford a wheelchair, so she had to crawl around using her hands. When Tatyana was six years old, Deborah McFadden, an American, visited the orphanage in Russia. She felt an instant connection with Tatyana, and she and her partner Bridget O'Shaughnessy adopted the little girl.

When she came to the USA, doctors said Tatyana was so ill that she did not have long to live. But she got better, and took part in a variety of sports to strengthen her muscles, such as swimming, gymnastics, and athletics.

In high school, she was not allowed to compete with athletes who did not have disabilities, and so had to race around an empty track on her own. Tatyana and her mother Deborah went to court, and Tatyana won the right to race at the same time as her fellow athletes.

You can't race!

I'll race you to court!

Tatyana was just a schoolgirl when she made her Paralympic debut at the age of 15, in Athens, Greece. She won a silver medal in the women's 100-m race and a bronze medal in the women's 200 m. At the 2008 Beijing Paralympic Games she added another three silvers and one bronze to her name.

In 2009 Tatyana entered the Chicago Marathon. As she specialized in shorter distance sprints, she thought it would be fun but didn't imagine she would do that well. She unexpectedly won, and finished so quickly that her mom still wasn't ready with the camera to film her victory!

In 2013, Tatyana became the first person, able-bodied or disabled, to win all four Grand Slam marathons (London, Boston, Chicago, and New York) in one year. At the World Championships in the same year, Tatyana won gold in every distance from 100 m to 5,000 m.

At the 2014 Winter Paralympic Games in Sochi, Russia, Tatyana won silver in cross-country skiing in front of her adoptive and birth mothers. This was a very meaningful moment for Tatyana. She said afterward it made her feel "fulfilled." In 2016, Tatyana won the Chicago, Boston, and London marathons once more, and took home four gold and two silver medals at the 2016 Rio Paralympics. She describes herself as "the fastest woman on three wheels!"

CHALLENGE YOURSELF LIKE TATYANA

Athletes like Tatyana are always trying to beat their own "personal best," and do better than they did before. They keep records of how well they do in each training session, and see if their performance is improving. Using a stopwatch, try recording and challenging your own personal best every few days over a few weeks (in running, or swimming, or another individual sport of your choice). It is important to make sure you are always testing yourself across the exact same time and distance to see if you are getting better.

KATIE LEDECKY

After only five years of competing internationally, Katie Ledecky had already become the most successful female swimmer of all time. She has won five Olympic gold medals, is a 14-time world champion, and holds three world records.

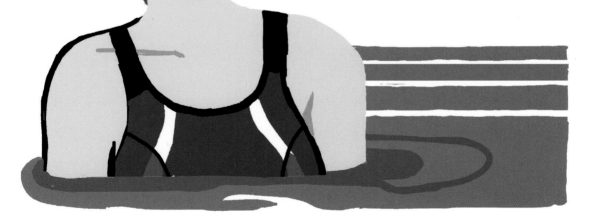

CHAMPION SWIMMER

Katie has broken 13 world records during her career, even without the recently banned high-tech swimsuits that allowed previous record holders to swim extra fast.

BORN: March 17, 1997

FROM: Washington, D.C. (USA)

COMPETED FOR: USA

Katie first joined a swim team at the age of six, encouraged by her nine-year-old brother. She always wanted to be in the same group as him, despite their age gap. By the time she was 13, she already had more speed and stamina than him—she could swim at a faster speed for 1,500 m than he could for 200 m.

Katie's parents have said that she has always been very strong-minded. At the age of six, her only goal was to finish a 25-m race without having to stop and rest on the way. Despite being told to pull out of a race because she had swimmer's ear, she demanded to be able to swim and achieved her goal of swimming the whole 25 m nonstop for the first time.

Katie made her international debut at the London 2012 Olympics and shocked the world when she won the 800-m freestyle at 15 years old with the second-fastest time ever recorded. At the Rio Olympics in 2016, she won four more gold medals, beating her fastest competitor by over 11 seconds in the 800-m freestyle.

She has won a total of 24 major international competitions. At one point she went undefeated in 13 straight individual international finals, often beating her opponents by vast distances. She has broken her own records time and time again in competitions. Katie's coaches say that her success comes from her mental strength, treating every distance like a sprint and giving her absolute best throughout a race. In addition, she gained a place at a top University in the USA.

SET GOALS LIKE KATIE

During her training for the 2016 Rio Olympics, Ledecky used a pull buoy—a training aid—printed with the numbers "56 5." Her coach later revealed that these numbers represented her goal times for Rio: 3 minutes 56 seconds for the 400-m freestyle and 8 minutes 5 seconds for the 800-m freestyle. She beat both these goals at Rio. Setting concrete goals like these for yourself can help you see progress clearly and stop you from getting disheartened. Break down a vague goal, like "I want to be great at swimming" into small, measurable steps along the way—for example, "I will complete four more lengths before stopping" or "I will complete a length two seconds faster."

MORE SPORTING HEROINES

The list of fast, strong, determined, and talented women in sports goes on and on. Here are some more brilliant women who have excelled through history, as well as some athletes who will no doubt be beating records into the future.

YUENÜ

LIVED: 5th century B.C.E.

BORN IN: Yue (China)

SPORTS: Sword fighting and archery

Yuenü, which means literally "The Lady of Yue," was a swordswoman and archer of legendary skill and wisdom. From a young age she hunted with her father and in this way learned how to use a sword and a bow. Yuenü developed her skills alone in the forest and based her techniques around the possibility of defeating multiple attackers. King Gouijan of Yue province called upon Yuenü to train his army for his planned war against another Chinese province. She explained that she thought of the sword as a door that can be divided into yin and yang. She believed in being outwardly calm, rather than putting energy into raging and showing off to an opponent. Instead, everything should be focused on internal strength, expressed in powerful, smooth movements, and precise, practiced footwork. These ideas were at the heart of Chinese martial arts for generations, and Yuenü is considered the first person in history to put forward these ideas.

LIS HARTEL

LIVED: March 14, 1921–February 12, 2009

BORN IN: Copenhagen (Denmark)

SPORT: Dressage

Lis Hartel became the Danish dressage champion in 1943 and again in 1944. Then, in September of 1944 she contracted polio and was initially almost entirely paralyzed. However, she didn't give up her favorite sport. She never regained the feeling below her knees, and at first fell off her horse many times even at a walking pace. But by 1947 she had improved so dramatically that she entered the Scandinavian Riding Championships and won second place. No one on the international scene knew about her paralysis. In the 1952 Helsinki Olympics, women were allowed to compete in dressage with the men for the first time. Lis could not mount or dismount without help, but still won silver. This incredible achievement also made her the first woman to ever win an Olympic medal in direct competition with men. Lis won another Olympic silver medal in dressage in 1956, and was the Danish dressage champion in 1952, 1953, 1954, 1956, and 1959. After retiring, she dedicated her life to supporting riding for people with disabilities and opened the first ever therapeutic riding center.

BILLIE JEAN KING

BORN: November 22, 1943

BORN IN: Long Beach, California (USA)

SPORT: Tennis

Billie Jean King took up tennis at age 11, learning to play at free local courts. Just four years later, she competed in her first Grand Slam. At the age of 17, in her first time at Wimbledon, she unexpectedly won the women's doubles title. Billie Jean went on to take her first Wimbledon singles title at 22, and to win the singles title six more times. In 1973, Billie Jean beat Bobby Riggs in an infamous $100,000 challenge match watched by a crowd of 30,000 and a TV audience of 50 million. Riggs, a former world number one in tennis, believed—wrongly—that he could beat the top female player in the world. Billie Jean has long fought for equality in sports, and founded the Women's Tennis Association and the Women's Sports Foundation. She came out as a lesbian in 1981, losing around $2 million in sponsorship deals. In 1987 she fell in love with her doubles partner, Ilana Kloss, and they are still together.

PATTI McGEE

BORN: August 23, 1945

BORN IN: Santa Monica, California (USA)

SPORT: Skateboarding

Patti McGee was the first female professional skateboarder and the first women's National Skateboarding Champion. She started skateboarding as a distraction when she was unable to surf. Her signature trick was the handstand, a move that made her the national champion, and a photograph of her doing the trick was used on the front cover of *Life* magazine. She was the first woman to be inducted into the Skateboarding Hall of Fame and the first woman to be on the cover of *Skateboarder* magazine. She set the world record at the time for "fastest girl on a skateboard," reaching 46 mph (75 kph). After becoming National Skateboarding Champion in 1965, she toured the USA for a year and was one of the first people to demonstrate skateboarding on national TV shows. Now in her seventies she still skates at local parks.

NICOLA ADAMS

BORN: October 26, 1982

BORN IN: Leeds (UK)

SPORT: Boxing

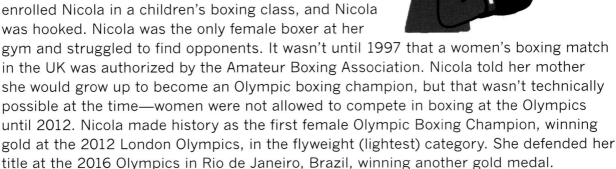

IMPOSSIBLE IS NOTHING

Nicola loved watching videos of boxing legend Muhammad Ali as a child. She got into boxing by accident when she was 12 years old. Her mom, who raised Nicola and her brother as a single parent, couldn't find a babysitter to watch them while she went to the gym. She enrolled Nicola in a children's boxing class, and Nicola was hooked. Nicola was the only female boxer at her gym and struggled to find opponents. It wasn't until 1997 that a women's boxing match in the UK was authorized by the Amateur Boxing Association. Nicola told her mother she would grow up to become an Olympic boxing champion, but that wasn't technically possible at the time—women were not allowed to compete in boxing at the Olympics until 2012. Nicola made history as the first female Olympic Boxing Champion, winning gold at the 2012 London Olympics, in the flyweight (lightest) category. She defended her title at the 2016 Olympics in Rio de Janeiro, Brazil, winning another gold medal.

KAORI ICHO

BORN: June 13, 1984

BORN IN: Hachinohe, Aomori (Japan)

SPORT: Freestyle wrestling

Kaori started wrestling around the age of four, encouraged by her older sister's passion for the sport. Kaori's training was very intense, as the culture of wrestling in Japan is incredibly tough. Athletes are encouraged to do exactly as their coach says, no matter the physical pain. Kaori won her first World Championship in 2002. Then for 13 years, between 2003 and 2016, she was undefeated over a total of 189 contests! She won nine World Championships and three Olympic gold medals during that time. After the shock of finally losing a match in January 2016, she bounced back to win a fourth Olympic gold medal in Rio only a few months later. Despite her success, Kaori is driven by trying to wrestle a perfect match rather than by breaking records and winning medals. This attitude has led to her being described as a samurai—a noble warrior—although she modestly says that she doesn't understand this label.

TIRUNESH DIBABA

BORN: June 1, 1985

BORN IN: Bekoji (Ethiopia)

SPORT: Long-distance runner

Tirunesh grew up with her family on their farm in Ethiopia. As a girl, she would run with buckets of water that she fetched from the river for her mother. She thinks this early training helped her be successful. She began running for sport when she moved to the capital city, Addis Ababa, at the age of 14. When she was 18 years old, Tirunesh became the youngest woman to win an individual gold medal in the 5,000 m at the 2003 World Championships. In 2005, she became the first woman to win both the 5,000-m and 10,000-m races in the World Championships. In 2007, she became the only woman to ever win back-to-back 10,000-m titles, when she managed to defend her title despite falling during the race. Because of her young age, she gained the nickname "the Baby-Faced Destroyer." Tirunesh has six Olympic medals, and has also won a total of 10 gold medals from the World Championships, World Cross Country Championships, and African Championships. Her 5,000-m record still stands as the world's fastest.

IBTIHAJ MUHAMMAD

BORN: December 4, 1985

BORN IN: Maplewood, New Jersey (USA)

SPORT: Fencing

Ibtihaj is the first American woman to ever wear a hijab (a headscarf that usually covers the head and chest) at the Olympics. She began fencing at the age of 13, choosing the sport partly because she was frustrated by having to alter the uniforms she wore for other sports to cover her arms and legs, in line with her religious beliefs about dressing modestly. The fencing uniform is designed to cover most of the body, to protect it against the jabbing end of the foil (sword). At the 2016 Rio Olympics, Ibtihaj won bronze in the team fencing competition, and became one of the first two Muslim-American women to ever win an Olympic medal. Dalilah Muhammad was the other, winning a gold medal in the 400-m hurdles at the same Olympic Games, but she received far less attention in the press because she didn't wear a hijab. Ibtihaj runs a clothing line for Muslim women who want to dress modestly but fashionably, and she works to promote sports and education for girls in the USA and other countries.

SIMONE BILES

BORN: March 14, 1997

BORN IN: Columbus, Ohio (USA)

SPORT: Gymnastics

Simone was adopted by her grandparents, as drug and alcohol addiction problems meant her mom and dad were unable to care for her and her siblings. At age six, Simone went on a field trip with her day care group to a gymnastics center. Little Simone watched the gymnasts and then tried to copy their moves. The instructors at the gym were amazed by her natural talent. She began training, and by the age of 10 she was competing nationally. At the age of 16, she won the all-around title at the World Championships. She went on to win the world title three times in a row. Then, at the 2016 Rio Olympics, she won four gold medals, making her the the most decorated (highest medal-earning) American gymnast of all time.

COUNTLESS OTHERS...

The women included in this book are just a few of the amazingly talented, determined, and downright revolutionary women in sports today and throughout the past. Some have made history and paved the way for women in sport; some continue to compete, win, and inspire all around the world today. All are true sporting champions. Will you be the next one to join their ranks?

GET INVOLVED IN SPORTS!

There are loads of different ways to get started with a new sport, or to take things further with a sport that you already play and love. Here are a few suggestions.

FIND A SPORTS CLUB, OR START ONE YOURSELF

You'd be amazed at all the different types of sports that you might be able to try out in your area. Have a look at what is available—your school or local athletic center should have some classes and clubs where you can learn something new or practice your skills, but you may also find local groups that run all sorts of different outdoor sports from kayaking to archery. If there isn't a club, start one yourself!

JUNIOR PARKRUNS

If running or wheelchair racing is your thing, then look into junior parkruns. Junior parkruns are free weekly 2-km runs that are open to all children and young people between the ages of 4 and 14. If you want to improve your fitness level, speed, or stamina for other sports, this is a great way to do it.

GO TO WATCH LIVE SPORTS

It can be really inspiring to see professionals competing in a sport that you love, or just think you might be interested in doing yourself. Most women's sports are cheaper to attend and watch than men's sports, and organizers really want to encourage young people to come along so you might find that you can watch it for free in many cases!

DISCOVER A NEW SPORT ONLINE

If you want to find out more about sports you haven't tried before, and learn how you could have a go yourself, try searching online. You can watch clips of sports on YouTube to inspire you, and find video tutorials for particular techniques.

45

GLOSSARY

Aboriginal A word used to describe indigenous people from mainland Australia and Tasmania.

Australian Open A major tennis tournament held every year in Melbourne, Australia.

Commonwealth Games An international sporting event held every four years, featuring athletes from the Commonwealth of Nations, which is a group of countries that used to be part of the British Empire.

Croix de Guerre A military medal awarded in France for acts of heroism involving combat with the enemy.

FIFA The international governing organization for soccer, which organizes big tournaments including the World Cup.

Grand Slam A set of major matches or tournaments in a particular sport in any given year.

Hijab A head covering worn in public by some Muslim women.

Indigenous (people) The people who first lived in a particular region, rather than people who arrived later in history from another place.

MBE/OBE British honors that are awarded to a person by the King or Queen for a particular achievement. An OBE (Order of the British Empire) is a higher honor than an MBE (Member of the Order of the British Empire).

Olympic Games The world's foremost sporting event featuring over 200 nations, held every four years. They began in the late 19th century but were inspired by the ancient Olympic Games, which was a sporting event held in Olympia, in ancient Greece.

Paralympic Games International sporting event for athletes with a range of disabilities, held every four years, immediately after the Olympic Games.

Polio An infectious disease that can cause paralysis.

Professional A person who does a sport as a paid job rather than as a hobby.

Stamina The physical or mental strength needed to do something difficult for long periods of time.

UEFA Europa League An annual soccer competition for European soccer clubs held since 1971.

Variety show An entertainment made up of multiple different acts, such as acrobatics, music, comedy, and juggling.

Yin and yang An idea from Chinese philosophy that says the world contains two forces, which are always opposite one another but also connected at the same time.

FURTHER INFORMATION

WEBSITES

Find out more about sports you haven't tried before on this BBC website.
bbc.co.uk/sport/get-inspired

Check out the Parkrun website for details of junior parkruns and wheelchair races around the UK and USA and see if there is an event near you.
parkrun.org.uk/events/juniorevents
parkrun.us/events/

Read inspiring stories and get some great ideas about different ways you can get active as part of the This Girl Can campaign. **www.thisgirlcan.co.uk**

BOOKS

Women in Sport by Rachel Ignotofsky (Wren and Rook, 2018)

Good Night Stories for Rebel Girls by Elena Favilli and Francesca Cavallo (Particular Books, 2017)

Olympic Expert by Paul Mason (Wayland, 2016)

Fantastically Great Women Who Changed the World by Kate Pankhurst (Bloomsbury, 2016)

INDEX

Aboriginal people 13–16
Adams, Nicola 40
African Championships 41
archery 37, 44
athletics 4, 9–11, 13–16, 29–32, 41
Australia 13–16

ballooning, hot-air 7
baseball 9–10
basketball 9–10
Biles, Simone 43
bobsledding 7
boxers 4, 7, 40
Brazil 20, 25–28, 32, 35–36, 40, 42–43
British Cycling National Track Championships 19

canoers 5–6
China 19, 31, 37
climbers 5, 7
Commonwealth Games 15, 19
Croix de Guerre 7
cyclists 4–5, 7–8, 17, 19–20

Denmark 38
Dibaba, Tirunesh 41
dressage 38

Ethiopia 41

fencing 42
FIFA Women's Cup 26
FIFA World Player of the Year 27
First World War 7
France 5–8
Freeman, Cathy 13–16

golfers 9–10, 12
Grand Slams (tennis) 23–24, 39
gymnastics 4, 30, 43

Hartel, Lis 38
hijab, wearing the 42
horse riding 38

ice skating 5, 7
Icho, Kaori 40

Japan 40

King, Billie Jean 39

Ledecky, Katie 33–36

McFadden, Tatyana 29–32
McGee, Patti 39
marathons 31–32
Marta 25–28
Marvingt, Marie 5–8
Medaille d'Or 8
Muhammad, Ibtihaj 42

National Skateboarding Champion 39

Olympic Games 11, 14–15, 18–19, 24, 33, 35–36, 38, 40–43

Para-cycling European Championships 19
Paralympians 17–20, 29–32
Paralympic Games 18–20, 31
people, indigenous 13–16

racers, wheelchair 29–32
runners 4, 13–16, 20, 32, 41, 45

skateboarding 4, 39
skiing 5, 7, 32
soccer players 3, 25–28
Storey, Sarah 17–20
swimming 4–6, 10, 17–20, 30, 32–36
sword fighting 4, 37

tennis 3–4, 10, 21–24, 39
Tour de France 5, 7

UEFA Europa League 27
UK 17–20, 31–32, 35, 39–40
USA 9–12, 15, 21–24, 29–36, 39, 42–43

Vieira da Silva, Marta 25–28
volleyball 10

Williams, Serena 21–24
Williams, Venus 21–24
Winter Paralympics 32
World Championships (athletics) 31, 41
World Championship (soccer) 26
World Championships (gymnastics) 43
World Championships (wrestling) 40
World Cross Country Championships 41
wrestling 40

Yuenü 37

Zaharias, Babe Didrikson 9–12

First edition for the United States and Canada published in 2018 by Barron's Educational Series, Inc.

Text © copyright 2018 by Georgia Amson-Bradshaw
Illustrated by Rita Petruccioli
Volume © copyright 2018 by Hodder and Stoughton
First published in Great Britain in 2018 by Wayland, an imprint of Hachette Children's Group, part of Hodder & Stoughton

The right of Georgia Amson-Bradshaw to be identified as the author of this work has been asserted by her in accordance with the Copyright, Designs, and Patent Act of 1988.

All inquiries should be addressed to:
Barron's Educational Series, Inc.
250 Wireless Boulevard
Hauppauge, NY 11788
www.barronseduc.com

Library of Congress Control No.: 2018939533

ISBN: 978-1-4380-1219-3

Date of Manufacture: May 2018
Manufactured by: WKT, Shenzhen, China

Printed in China
9 8 7 6 5 4 3 2 1